Guide to Reading and Writing Japanese

Written by
Mamori Sugita Hughes

LIVING LANGUAGE®

Published in the United States by Living Language, an imprint of Random House, Inc.

www.livinglanguage.com

Editor: Suzanne McQuade
Production Editor: Ciara Robinson
Production Manager: Tom Marshall
Interior Design: Sophie Chin
Illustrations: Nanako Inoue

First Edition

ISBN: 978-0-307-97178-4

This book is available at special discounts for bulk purchases for sales promotions or premiums. Special editions, including personalized covers, excerpts of existing books, and corporate imprints, can be created in large quantities for special needs. For more information, write to Special Markets/ Premium Sales, 1745 Broadway, MD 3-1, New York, New York 10019 or e-mail specialmarkets@ randomhouse.com.

PRINTED IN THE UNITED STATES OF AMERICA

10 9 8 7 6 5

Acknowledgments

Thanks to the Living Language team: Amanda D'Acierno, Christopher Warnasch, Suzanne McQuade, Laura Riggio, Erin Quirk, Heather Dalton, Amanda Munoz, Fabrizio LaRocca, Siobhan O'Hare, Sophie Chin, Pat Stango, Sue Daulton, Alison Skrabek, Ciara Robinson, Andrea McLin, and Tom Marshall.

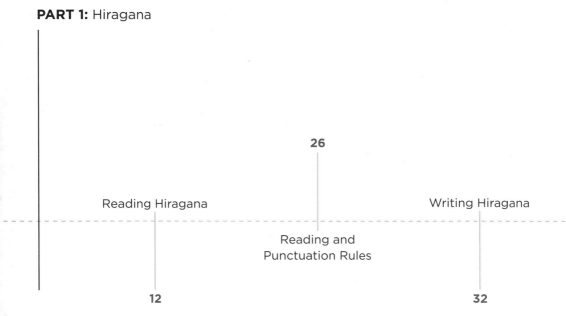
COURSE

PART 2: Katakana

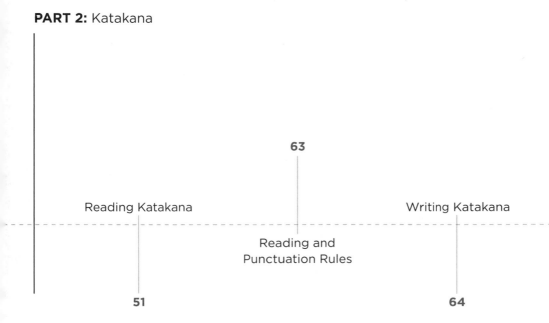

OUTLINE

PART 3: Kanji

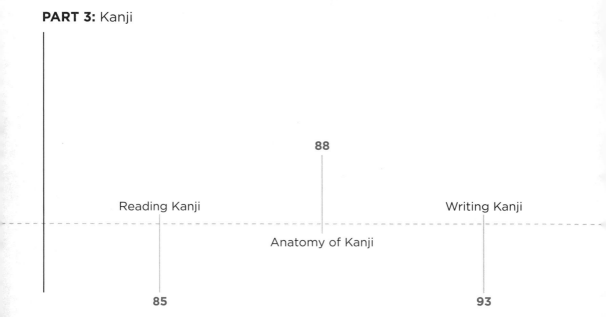

Reading Kanji

88

Anatomy of Kanji

Writing Kanji

85

93

Overview of the Japanese Writing System

The Japanese writing system consists of three types of symbols: ひらがな hiragana, カタカナ katakana, and 漢字 kanji. Each type of symbol is used for specific purposes. In this guide, we'll look at each type of symbol individually, and teach you how to read and write in Japanese. First, an overview of the types of symbols.

カタカナ Katakana

There are 46 カタカナ katakana symbols. Katakana is used mainly to write words and names of foreign origin. It is also used to write words that express sounds (i.e. onomatopoeia) such as the equivalent of the English *meow* and *cuckoo*. Occasionally, katakana is used to place emphasis on a word of Japanese origin. Just as with the English alphabet, katakana characters are phonetic symbols, which is to say that each character represents a specific sound. What makes katakana characters distinct from the English alphabet is that each katakana character represents a syllable. In other words, katakana represents either a vowel ([a], [i], [u], [e], [o]) or a combination of a consonant and a vowel (e.g. [sa], [ke]).

バ　ナ　ナ *banana*
[ba] [na] [na]

漢字 Kanji

漢字 Kanji refers to a set of Chinese characters and is used for content words such as nouns, verbs, and adjectives. Kanji was originally borrowed from the Chinese language and adapted to fit the Japanese language. While the Japanese adopted the Chinese way of reading the kanji characters, they also assigned Japanese readings in order to match the characters to existing Japanese words.

Therefore, each kanji character usually has at least two possible readings. The appropriate reading of a particular character depends on its usage. Each kanji character carries a specific meaning.

三 (*three*) + 人 (*person*) = 三人 **sannin** (*three people*)

学 (*learn*) + 生 (*life*) = 学生 **gakusee** (*student*)

朝 (*morning*) + 食 (*eat*) = 朝食 **chooshoku** (*breakfast*)

There are 1,945 *Kanji Characters in Common Use* (常用漢字 **Jooyoo Kanji**) announced officially by the Japanese Ministry of Education. In publications aimed at Japanese adults such as books and newspapers, knowledge of these 1,945 characters is assumed. There are also a good number of less frequently used characters.

ひらがな Hiragana

Hiragana is the most basic type of symbols in Japanese. Just as katakana, hiragana consists of forty-six characters; they are phonetic and syllabic symbols. Everything that is not represented in katakana or kanji is written in hiragana. This includes, but is not limited to, function words such as particles and inflectional endings. Hiragana is also used when one chooses not to use kanji to write particular words. This usually happens when the writer or reader's knowledge of kanji is limited, or when the particular kanji character is not one of *the Kanji Characters in Common Use* (常用漢字 **Jooyoo Kanji**).

い ぬ *dog*
[i] [nu]

The word **inu** (*dog*) can be written in kanji, but if you choose to write it in hiragana, it looks like the above.

かな Kana vs. 漢字 Kanji

Hiragana and katakana are referred to collectively as かな **kana**, to distinguish them from kanji. Japanese children are taught kana first, then they start learning kanji in elementary school at the age of six or seven. Because there are so many kanji, it is taught all the way up through high school.

Japanese Text at a Glance

Now that you know how hiragana, katakana, and kanji are used for different purposes, let's take a look at a full sentence in which all the three types of symbols are used.

私はアメリカ人です。
Watashi wa amerika jin desu.
I am an American.

Let's break it down now to see how the different types of symbols work together.

私/は/アメリカ/人/です。
[**watashi**]/[**wa**]/[**amerika**]/[**jin**]/[**desu**]
I/the particle wa/*America/person/be (period)*
kanji/hiragana/katakana/kanji/hiragana

As you can see, katakana is used for the word that reads [**amerika**], which is borrowed from the English word *America*. **Kanji** is used for the words that mean *I* and *person*. Hiragana is used for the particle は **wa** and the present tense polite form of the copula (whose English equivalent is the verb *be*). Essentially, kanji is used for content words, while hiragana is used for function words.

Direction of Writing

Japanese may be written horizontally from left to right just like English, or vertically from top to bottom and right to left. Look at the two examples below and note the differences between the horizontal writing (on the left) and the vertical writing (on the right). Note especially the placement of punctuation.

土曜日はよく経済学のセミナーに出ますが、日曜日はリラックスします。たまにお昼まで寝ます。それから午後は時々小説や雑誌を読みます。今、村上春樹の「海辺のカフカ」を読んでいます。

土曜日はよく経済学のセミナーに出ますが、日曜日はリラックスします。たまにお昼まで寝ます。それから午後は時々小説や雑誌を読みます。今、村上春樹の「海辺のカフカ」を読んでいます。

Vertical writing is used in most published works such as newspapers and books, with the exception of science books and some types of magazines. Vertical writing used to be predominant in other areas as well such as letters and manuscripts, but horizontal writing has become more common for everyday writing, partly due to the now widespread use of personal computers. Throughout these coursebooks, you will see only horizontal writing used.

ふりがな Furigana

Since there are a significant number of kanji characters, many readers need some guidance on how to read them in text. There is a reading aid called ふりがな furigana, which is basically small kana printed next to or above kanji to indicate its pronunciation. In horizontal text, furigana is placed above the line of text. In vertical text, it is placed to the right of the line of text. Furigana is most commonly used in materials for Japanese children and learners of Japanese as a foreign language. You will see furigana used throughout the coursebooks in this package. Furigana may be also used over kanji which are not among *the Kanji Characters in Common Use* (常用漢字 **Jooyoo Kanji**) in materials aimed at adult Japanese speakers. Since kanji used in names (of people, places, etc.) are sometimes pronounced in uncommon ways, you will often see furigana over names and addresses when someone is filling out forms.

<ruby>私<rt>わたし</rt></ruby>は<ruby>学生<rt>がくせい</rt></ruby>です。

Watashi wa gakusee desu.

I am a student.

Part 1: Hiragana

Reading Hiragana

THE BASIC HIRAGANA CHARACTERS

THE HIRAGANA CHART

The following chart shows what is called ごじゅうおん **gojuuon**, which literally means *fifty sounds*. However, the modern system actually consists of only forty-six sounds. The chart is read from top to bottom and right to left. This is the order in which words are given in a dictionary.

ひらがなのごじゅうおんひょう **Hiragana no gojuuon hyoo** *The hiragana chart*

	w	r	y	m	h	n	t	s	k	a	
ん n	わ wa	ら ra	や ya	ま ma	は ha	な na	た ta	さ sa	か ka	あ a	**a**
		り ri		み mi	ひ hi	に ni	ち chi	し shi	き ki	い i	**i**
		る ru	ゆ yu	む mu	ふ fu	ぬ nu	つ tsu	す su	く ku	う u	**u**
		れ re		め me	へ he	ね ne	て te	せ se	け ke	え e	**e**
	を o	ろ ro	よ yo	も mo	ほ ho	の no	と to	そ so	こ ko	お o	**o**

Each hiragana character represents either a vowel or a consonant-vowel combination. One exception is the character ん **n**. However, this sound is considered a single syllable in Japanese. Therefore, we can say that every hiragana character represents a syllable.

HIRAGANA CHARACTERS ONE BY ONE

Let's go through all the hiragana characters in the chart one by one, in the order you would find them in a dictionary. The first five characters are vowels corresponding to the far-right column in the hiragana chart. This column is called あぎょう **agyoo** *the A-line.*

あぎょう **agyoo** *the A-line*	
あ a	ありがとうございます。 **Arigatoo gozaimasu.** *Thank you.*
い i	はい。 **Hai.** *Yes.*
う u	うち **uchi** *home*
え e	おなまえは？ **Onamae wa?** *What's your name?*
お o	おなまえは？ **Onamae wa?** *What's your name?*

The rest of the characters represent combinations of consonants and vowels. The first column after あぎょう **agyoo** *the A-line* combines the consonant **k** and the vowels. This column is called かぎょう **kagyoo** *the Ka-line.*

かぎょう **kagyoo** *the Ka-line*	
か ka	たなかさん **Tanaka san** *Mr./Ms. Tanaka*
き ki	げんきです。 **Genki desu.** *I'm fine.*
く ku	がくせい **gakusee** *student*
け ke	とけい **tokee** *watch/clock*
こ ko	おとこ **otoko** *male*

The next column is さぎょう sagyoo *the Sa-line*:

さぎょう sagyoo *the Sa-line*	
さ sa	さようなら。**Sayoonara.** *Goodbye.*
し shi	どうぞよろしく。**Doozo yoroshiku.** *Nice to meet you.*
す su	〜です。**… desu.** *to be …*
せ se	せんせい **sensee** *teacher*
そ so	それではまた。**Sorede wa mata.** *See you later.*

Please note that the combination of the consonant s and the vowel i results in the sound **shi** in Japanese, not **si**. Japanese does not have the sound **si**.

The next column is たぎょう tagyoo *the Ta-line*:

たぎょう tagyoo *the Ta-line*	
た ta	たなかさん **Tanaka san** *Mr./Ms. Tanaka*
ち chi	ちち **chichi** *father (one's own)*
つ tsu	くつ **kutsu** *shoes*
て te	はじめまして。**Hajimemashite.** *How do you do?*
と to	ひと **hito** *person*

Please note that the combination of the consonant t and the vowel i results in the sound **chi** not **ti**. Likewise, the combination of the t and u results in the sound **tsu**, not **tu**.

Let's look at the rest of the characters.

なぎょう nagyoo *the Na-line*	
な na	おなまえは? **Onamae wa?** *What's your name?*
に ni	あに **ani** *older brother (one's own)*
ぬ nu	いぬ **inu** *dog*
ね ne	あね **ane** *older sister (one's own)*
の no	おんなのひと **onna no hito** *woman*

はぎょう hagyoo *the Ha-line*	
は ha	はち hachi *eight*
ひ hi	ひらがな hiragana *hiragana*
ふ fu	ふたり futari *two people*
へ he	へや heya *room*
ほ ho	ほん hon *book*

Please note that the combination of **h** and **u** in Japanese results in **fu**, not **hu**.

まぎょう magyoo *the Ma-line*	
ま ma	います imasu *to have, there is, to exist*
み mi	おやすみなさい。 Oyasuminasai. *Good night.*
む mu	むすこ musuko *son (one's own)*
め me	ごめんなさい。 Gomennasai. *I'm sorry.*
も mo	いもうと imooto *younger sister (one's own)*

やぎょう yagyoo *the Ya-line*	
や ya	おやすみなさい。 Oyasuminasai. *Good night.*
ゆ yu	しょうゆ shooyu *soy sauce*
よ yo	ようこそ。 Yookoso. *Welcome.*

As you can see, there are only three characters in やぎょう **yagyoo** *the Ya-line*.

らぎょう ragyoo *the Ra-line*	
ら ra	ひらがな hiragana *hiragana*
り ri	ありがとうございます。 Arigatoo gozaimasu. *Thank you.*
る ru	くるま kuruma *car*
れ re	れい ree *zero*
ろ ro	ろく roku *six*

わぎょう wagyoo *the Wa-line*	
わ wa	わたし watashi *I*
を o	を o *the particle o*

There are only two characters in わぎょう **wagyoo** *the Wa-line*. Please note that the character を is pronounced **o**, not **wo**. In modern Japanese, this character is used only to write the particle を **o**, whose function is to mark an object in a sentence, as in すしをたべます。**Sushi o tabemasu.** *I eat sushi.*

And now, here's the final hiragana character, ん **n**, which does not belong to any "line."

ん n	こんばんは。**Konban wa.** *Good evening.*

The character ん is also special because it represents a single consonant sound, as opposed to a combination of consonant + vowel.

DIACRITICS AND SPECIAL CHARACTER COMBINATIONS

In addition to the forty-six sounds that you've just learned, additional sounds are created through the use of diacritics and specific combinations of the basic characters. We'll guide you through these characters in the following sections.

DIACRITICS

There are two types of diacritics used over some of the basic hiragana characters: だくてん **dakuten** and はんだくてん **handakuten**. だくてん **Dakuten** turns voiceless consonants into voiced consonants; はんだくてん **handakuten** turns voiced consonants into voiceless consonants. The difference between voiced and voiceless consonants is the presence or absence of vibration. To see what this means, put your fingers on your throat while pronouncing the English sound

g. You should feel vibration. This is because your vocal chords vibrate when you pronounce g, which is a voiced consonant. In contrast, if you pronounce a voiceless consonant k, you won't feel vibration. The tongue position and the shape of the lips for pronouncing k is the same as pronouncing g. The only difference between them is the presence or absence of vibration.

The voiceless consonants can be made into voiced consonants by the use of a two-dot symbol called **dakuten** (formal) or てんてん **tenten** (informal). **Dakuten** is placed to the upper right of the characters in かぎょう **kagyoo** *the Ka-line*, さぎょう **sagyoo** *the Sa-line*, たぎょう **tagyoo** *the Ta-line*, and はぎょう **hagyoo** *the Ha-line*.

The use of だくてん **dakuten**

k	g	s	z	t	d	h	b
か ka	が ga	さ sa	ざ za	た ta	だ da	は ha	ば ba
き ki	ぎ gi	し shi	じ ji	ち chi	ぢ ji	ひ hi	び bi
く ku	ぐ gu	す su	ず zu	つ tsu	づ zu	ふ fu	ぶ bu
け ke	げ ge	せ se	ぜ ze	て te	で de	へ he	べ be
こ ko	ご go	そ so	ぞ zo	と to	ど do	ほ ho	ぼ bo

Note that ず and づ share the same pronunciation **zu**. They are, however, not interchangeable. For example, the word that means *number* must always be written with ず as in かず **kazu**, but not かづ. Likewise, the word that means *bridle* or *reins* must always be written with づ as in たづな **tazuna**, but not たずな. It is, however, the case that ず is used much more often than づ in Japanese words.

You may also have noticed that じ **ji** and ぢ **ji** have the same pronunciation. However, the character ぢ is used only in a few words, and the sound **ji** is represented by the character じ most of the time.

Let's look at each of the above characters with **dakuten** one by one with an example.

がぎょう gagyoo *the Ga-line*	
が ga	がくせい gakusee *student*
ぎ gi	ぎんこう ginkoo *bank*
ぐ gu	かぐ kagu *furniture*
げ ge	ほうげん hoogen *dialect*
ご go	えいご eego *English (language)*

ざぎょう zagyoo *the Za-line*	
ざ za	ざっし zasshi *magazine*
じ ji	じかん jikan *time*
ず zu	かず kazu *number*
ぜ ze	かぜ kaze *wind*
ぞ zo	ぞう zoo *elephant*

だぎょう dagyoo *the Da-line*	
だ da	だいく daiku *carpenter*
ぢ ji	はなぢ hanaji *nose bleed*
づ zu	おこづかい okozukai *allowance*
で de	でんしゃ densha *train*
ど do	どく doku *poison*

ばぎょう bagyoo *the Ba-line*	
ば ba	おばあさん obaasan *grandmother (someone else's)*
び bi	びん bin *bottle*
ぶ bu	ぶた buta *pig*
べ be	べんきょう benkyoo *study*
ぼ bo	そぼ sobo *grandmother (one's own)*

The following pairs of examples illustrate the contrast between words with voiceless consonants and words with voiced consonants:

Word without だくてん dakuten	Word with だくてん dakuten
とく toku *virtue*	どく doku *poison*
せん sen *thousand*	ぜん zen *Zen Buddhism*
か ka *mosquito*	が ga *moth*
ふた futa *lid*	ぶた buta *pig*

You may have noticed that the way you pronounce the voiced ば ba び bi ぶ bu べ be ぼ bo is different from the voiceless は ha ひ hi ふ fu へ he ほ ho. The sounds ば ba び bi ぶ bu べ be ぼ bo use both lips (this is called "bilabial"), but when you pronounce は ha ひ hi ふ fu へ he ほ ho, your lips do not touch at all. In order to represent voiceless bilabial sounds, a small circle called はんだくてん handakuten (formal) or まる maru (informal) is placed to the upper right of each of the characters は ha ひ hi ふ fu へ he ほ ho, as shown in the following chart.

The use of はんだくてん handakuten

h	p
は ha	ぱ pa
ひ hi	ぴ pi
ふ fu	ぷ pu
へ he	ぺ pe
ほ ho	ぽ po

Let's look at the five characters with **handakuten** one by one with some examples below.

ぱぎょう pagyoo *the Pa-line*	
ぱ pa	いっぱい ippai *one (glass/bowl/cup)*
ぴ pi	いっぴき ippiki *one (animal)*
ぷ pu	いっぷん ippun *one minute*

ぱぎょう pagyoo the Pa-line	
ペ pe	いっぺん ippen sudden change
ぽ po	いっぽん ippon one (long and thin object)

Compare the following three words; the first one with ひ **hi** (no diacritic), the second one with び **bi** (with **dakuten**), and the third one with ぴ **pi** (with **handakuten**).

no diacritics	with **dakuten**	with **handakuten**
ひん **hin** dignity	びん **bin** bottle	ぴん **pin** pin
(Note that since the word ぴん **pin** comes from the English word *pin*, it is normally written in katakana, which you'll learn in the next chapter.)		

GLIDES

A glide is a sound that contains a consonant and y, such as **kya**. Glides are written with the combination of **hiragana** characters containing the vowel i and small や **ya**, ゆ **yu**, or よ **yo**. There are thirty-six combination characters that represent gliding sound.

p	b	d	z	g	r	m	h	n	t	s	k	
ぴゃ	びゃ	ぢゃ	じゃ	ぎゃ	りゃ	みゃ	ひゃ	にゃ	ちゃ	しゃ	きゃ	**ya**
pya	bya	ja	ja	gya	rya	mya	hya	nya	cha	sha	kya	
ぴゅ	びゅ	ぢゅ	じゅ	ぎゅ	りゅ	みゅ	ひゅ	にゅ	ちゅ	しゅ	きゅ	**yu**
pyu	byu	ju	ju	gyu	ryu	myu	hyu	nyu	chu	shu	kyu	
ぴょ	びょ	ぢょ	じょ	ぎょ	りょ	みょ	ひょ	にょ	ちょ	しょ	きょ	**yo**
pyo	byo	jo	jo	gyo	ryo	myo	hyo	nyo	cho	sho	kyo	

Now, let's look at each of the above combinations along with an example of a word using each glide.

きゃ kya	きゃく **kyaku** customer
きゅ kyu	きゅう **kyuu** nine
きょ kyo	きょうだい **kyoodai** siblings
しゃ sha	いしゃ **isha** medical doctor

しゅ shu	こんしゅう konshuu *this week*
しょ sho	しょうゆ shooyu *soy sauce*
ちゃ cha	おちゃ ocha *Japanese tea*
ちゅ chu	ちゅうしょく chuushoku *lunch*
ちょ cho	ちょうしょく chooshoku *breakfast*
にゃ nya	こんにゃく konnyaku *Konnyaku potato*
にゅ nyu	とうにゅう toonyuu *soy milk*
にょ nyo	によう nyoo *urine*
ひゃ hya	ひゃく hyaku *hundred*
ひゅ hyu	ひゅう hyuu *onomatopoeia representing the sound of blowing wind*
ひょ hyo	ひょうげん hyoogen *expression*
みゃ mya	みゃく myaku *pulse*
みゅ myu	*word example not available*
みょ myo	みょう myoo *strange*
りゃ rya	りゃくご ryakugo *abbreviation*
りゅ ryu	りゅう ryuu *dragon*
りょ ryo	りょうり ryoori *cooking*
ぎゃ gya	ぎゃく gyaku *opposite*
ぎゅ gyu	ぎゅうにく gyuuniku *beef*
ぎょ gyo	しょくぎょう shokugyoo *occupation*
じゃ ja	じゃま jama *intrusion*
じゅ ju	じゅう juu *ten*
じょ jo	てんじょう tenjoo *ceiling*
ぢゃ ja	めおとぢゃわん meotojawan *"his and hers" rice bowl set*
ぢゅ ju	*word example not available*
ぢょ jo	いっぽんぢょうし ipponjooshi *monotonous*

びゃ bya	びゃくや byakuya *white night*
びゅ byu	ごびゅう gobyuu *error (fml.)*
びょ byo	びょういん byooin *hospital*
ぴゃ pya	はっぴゃく happyaku *eight hundred*
ぴゅ pyu	ぴゅう pyuu *onomatopoeia representing the sound of blowing wind*
ぴょ pyo	はっぴょう happyoo *presentation*

Note that each of the phonetic notations for glides does not necessarily contain the alphabet character **y**, such as ちゃ **cha** and しゅ **shu**. However, if you pronounce them, you'll hear the sound **y**.

You may have noticed that じゃ **ja** and ぢゃ **ja** have the same pronunciation. The same goes for, じゅ **ju** and ぢゅ **ju**, じょ **jo** and ぢょ **jo**. However, they are not interchangeable. For example, the word that means *ten* must always be written with じゅ as in じゅう, but not ぢゅう.

Some of the character combinations above are rarely used; you see that some word examples are missing in the above chart. Furthermore, some of the examples above aren't really everyday words (such as めおとぢゃわん **meotojawan**, いっぽんぢょうし **ipponjooshi**, ごびゅう **gobyuu**). These words are only listed for the purpose of exemplifying the sound; you do not have to learn them closely.

Each of the combination characters above has the value of one syllable. In contrast, when two characters are written in the same size, you would have two syllables. For example, しゃ **sha** has only one syllable, but しや **shiya** has two. It is very important that the characters や **ya**, ゆ **yu**, and よ **yo** in glides are written small. If written big, it may result in a completely different word. Here are some examples:

With a glide			Without a glide		
きゃく	kyaku	*customer*	きやく	kiyaku	*agreement, rules*
きょう	kyoo	*today*	きよう	kiyoo	*promotion, appointment*
ひゃく	hyaku	*hundred*	ひやく	hiyaku	*leap*
りゅう	ryuu	*dragon*	りゆう	riyuu	*reason*
じゅう	juu	*ten*	じゆう	jiyuu	*freedom*

DOUBLE CONSONANTS

A double consonant can be recognized by a brief pause between sounds within a word, such as がっこう **gakkoo** *school*. When you have double consonants, the consonant of the second syllable (**k** in がっこう **gakkoo**) has the duration of one syllable. Double consonants are written with a small つ **tsu** placed immediately before the consonant to be doubled. The consonants that can be doubled are **k**, **s**, **t**, **c**, and **p**. Below are some examples:

Double Consonants	
k	がっこう **gakkoo** *school*
s	いっさつ **issatsu** *one (book, magazine)*
s	いっしょに **issho ni** *together*
t	みっつ **mittsu** *three (native Japanese number)*
c	まっちゃ **maccha** *matcha green tea*
p	すっぱい **suppai** *sour*

Compare the following pairs of examples. The first word in each pair has double consonants, while the second word does not. However, all of the examples below are three-syllable words.

With a double consonant	Without a double consonant
かって **katte** *selfish*	かつて **katsute** *formerly*
はっか **hakka** *ignition*	はつか **hatsuka** *the 20th day of a month*

With a double consonant	Without a double consonant
ねっき **nekki** *hot air*	ねつき **netsuki** *falling asleep*

Keep in mind that double **n** are not considered double consonants. This is because the first **n** is represented by the character ん **n**, as illustrated in the following examples:

さんにん	sannin	*three people*
どんな	donna	*what kind of*

LONG VOWELS

Long vowels are created by two of the same vowel appearing consecutively in a single word. Each of the two vowels retains the same length and quality. However, keep in mind that the two vowels are pronounced as a continuous sound (thus creating a long vowel), but not as two separate vowels. The following chart shows all the character combinations that create long vowels.

Long Vowels										
w	**r**	**y**	**m**	**h**	**n**	**t**	**s**	**k**	**a**	
わあ waa	らあ raa	やあ yaa	まあ maa	はあ haa	なあ naa	たあ taa	さあ saa	かあ kaa	ああ aa	**aa**
	りい rii		みい mii	ひい hii	にい nii	ちい chii	しい shii	きい kii	いい ii	**ii**
	るう ruu	ゆう yuu	むう muu	ふう fuu	ぬう nuu	つう tsuu	すう suu	くう kuu	うう uu	**uu**
	れい ree		めい mee	へい hee	ねえ ねい nee	てい tee	せい see	けい kee	ええ えい ee	**ee**
	ろう roo	よう yoo	もう moo	ほう ほお hoo	のう noo	とお とう too	そう soo	こお こう koo	おお おう oo	**oo**

As you can see in the charts above, different character combinations sometimes share an identical sound. For example, おう **oo** and おお **oo**, こう **koo** and

こお **koo**. Notice that the second vowel in the sequence **ee** is often written with the character い **i** instead of え **e**. Likewise, the second vowel in the sequence **oo** is often written with the character う **u** instead of お **o**. When you see these combinations, make sure that you pronounce them correctly.

Following are some example words that contain long vowels:

いいえ	**iie**	*no*
えいが	**eega**	*movie*
おおきい	**ookii**	*big*
おかあさん	**okaasan**	*mother (someone else's)*
とけい	**tokee**	*watch, clock*
こうこうせい	**kookoosee**	*high school student*
せんせい	**sensee**	*teacher*
バスてい	**basutee**	*bus stop*
おとうさん	**otoosan**	*father (someone else's)*
おにいさん	**oniisan**	*older brother (someone else's)*
おねえさん	**oneesan**	*older sister (someone else's)*
ほうこう	**hookoo**	*direction*
せつめい	**setsumee**	*description*
いもうと	**imooto**	*younger sister (one's own)*
れい	**ree**	*zero*
ろうか	**rooka**	*hallway*

Long vowels can be created with hiragana containing diacritics and glides as well. Below are some examples:

ぐうぜん	**guuzen**	*coincidence*
れいぞうこ	**reezooko**	*refrigerator*
じゅう	**juu**	*ten*
こんしゅう	**konshuu**	*this week*
きょう	**kyoo**	*today*

おめでとうございます! **Omedetoogozaimasu!** *Congratulations!* You've learned all the basic hiragana characters, diacritics, and special character combinations. In the next section, you'll learn some special reading and punctuation rules.

READING AND PUNCTUATION RULES

In this section, you'll learn some important rules when you read Japanese sentences and passages, including:

☐ Special reading of particles

☐ Reading phrases and sentences

☐ Spacing

☐ Punctuation marks

Special Reading of Particles

THE PARTICLE は WA

The particle wa is written not with the character わ, but with the character は. Note that expressions of greeting such as こんにちは konnichi wa *hello* and こんばんは konban wa *good evening* also contain the character は, and it is pronounced wa. This is because the origin of the phrase こんにちは konnichi wa is "こんにち konnichi *today* + the particle は wa"; and likewise the origin of the phrase こんばんは konban wa is "こんばん konban *this evening* + the particle は wa." There are other fixed expressions such as それではまた sorede wa mata *see you later* and ではありません de wa arimasen *to not be* whose wa sounds are all originated from the particle は wa. In those cases too, the character は is pronounced wa.

わたしはにほんじんです。	Watashi wa nihonjin desu.	*I am Japanese.*
やまださんはがくせいではありません。	Yamada san wa gakusee de wa arimasen.	*Mr./Ms. Yamada is not a student.*
こんにちは。	Konnichi wa.	*Hello./Good afternoon.*
それではまた。	Sorede wa mata.	*See you later.*

THE PARTICLE へ E

The particle e is optionally used (instead of the particle に ni) along with verbs that express directional movement, such as いきます ikimasu (*to go*) and かえります kaerimasu (*to to home*). The particle e must be written with the character へ, but not with え.

がっこうへいきます。	Gakkoo e ikimasu.	*I'm going to school.*
うちへかえります。	Uchi e kaerimasu.	*I'm going home.*

THE PARTICLE を O

The particle **o**, whose main function is to mark an object in a sentence, must be written with the character を, but not with お. This is the only usage for the character を.

すしをたべます。	Sushi o tabemasu.	*I eat sushi.*
ほんをよみます。	Hon o yomimasu.	*I read books.*

READING PHRASES AND SENTENCES

When there are identical vowels across words or phrases in a sentence, they are not considered to form a long vowel. Therefore, the second vowel must be articulated; do not pronounce the two vowels as a continuous sound. For example, in あねとおとうと **ane to otooto** *older sister and younger brother*, the third character と **to** and the fourth character お **o** are not part of a single word; と **to** is a particle, and お **o** is the first character in the word おとうと **otooto** *younger brother*. Therefore, と **to** and お **o** must be pronounced separately, instead of a continuous **too**. On the other hand, the fifth character と **to** and the sixth character う **u** are part of a single word おとうと **otooto**. Therefore, とう **too** is considered to contain a long vowel, and you have to pronounce the two vowels **oo** consecutively.

がくせいがふたりいます。	Gakusee ga futari imasu.	*There are two students.*
がくせいではありません。	Gakusee de wa arimasen.	*I am not a student.*
いえへかえります。	Ie e kaerimasu.	*I'm going home.*
ほんがあります。	Hon ga arimasu.	*There is a book.*

Spacing

In everyday Japanese text, where both かな kana and かんじ kanji are used, spaces are not placed between words, because character alternations visually provide separations between lexical words and functional parts of speech (such as particles and verb endings).

私は日本語を勉強します。	Watashi wa nihongo o benkyooshimasu.	I study Japanese.

However, when ひらがな hiragana is used exclusively, or when few かんじ kanji characters are used, spaces can be provided to make it easier to read. Spaces should be used between phrases. A space should never separate a particle from the word that it attaches to.

わたしは　にほんごを　べんきょうします。
Watashi wa nihongo o benkyooshimasu.
I study Japanese.

A note on spacing when you write phonetic representations of Japanese in the Roman alphabet: most Japanese speakers would put a space between phrases, such as in **Yamadasanwa kyoo sushio tabemasu** *Mr./Ms. Yamada eats sushi today*. On the other hand, linguists would use more spaces to separate all parts of speech, such as in **Yamada san wa kyoo sushi o tabemasu**. There is no single "correct" way to transcribe Japanese with the Roman alphabet; you may even see different versions across different Japanese textbooks. Thus, you do not have to worry too much about where to put spaces. Just think of the ease of reading. Apparently, if there is no space in a sentence, it is very difficult to read and you want to avoid that!

Punctuation Marks

くてん KUTEN **PERIOD** 。

くてん **Kuten** (formal) or まる **maru** (informal), which is a small circle, is used to mark the end of a sentence. Note that it also marks the end of a question, instead of a question mark.

こんにちは。	Konnichi wa.	*Hello./Good afternoon.*
がくせいですか。	Gakusee desu ka.	*Are you a student?*

とうてん TOOTEN **COMMA** 、

Rules for the use of とうてん **tooten** (formal) or てん **ten** (informal) are much looser than English rules for using commas. They may be placed wherever a natural break in the sentence might occur. An example of a common place you'd see a comma is right after a subordinate clause (such as a *when* clause and a *while* clause). You should keep in mind that とうてん **tooten** should not be placed immediately before a particle or conjunction.

おとうとはがくせいですが、あにはせんせいです。	Otooto wa gakusee desu ga, ani wa sensee desu.	*While my younger brother is a student, my older brother is a teacher.*
にほんにいったとき、すしをたべました。	Nihon ni itta toki, sushi o tabemashita.	*When I went to Japan, I ate sushi.*

かぎかっこ KAGIKAKKO **QUOTATION MARKS** 「 」

かぎかっこ **Kagikakko** are placed to the upper left of the first character and lower right of the last character in horizontal writing.

「こんばんは。」	"Konban wa."	*"Good evening."*

かっこ KAKKO **PARENTHESES**（）

The usage of かっこ **kakko** is basically identical to that of parentheses in English text. Additionally, it is sometimes used to indicate the reading of kanji when furigana is not possible due to, for example, the lack of functionality in the word-processing equipment or if the font size is too small to use furigana.

私（わたし）の名前（なまえ）は山田（やまだ）です。	Watashi (watashi) no namae (namae) wa Yamada (Yamada) desu.	*My name is Yamada.*

なみせん NAMISEN **WAVE DASH** 〜

なみせん **Namisen** is mainly used to indicate duration such as *five o'clock to seven o'clock* or *Monday through Friday*. This usage corresponds to the English *en dash* (-). When you read なみせん **namisen** aloud in this usage, you'll say から **kara**, which means *from*. なみせん **Namisen** is also used to indicate ellipses. This usage is often seen in Japanese language text books where new verbs are introduced together with appropriate particles to be used with. This usage corresponds to the English ellipses mark "… ".

5:00〜7:00	goji kara shichiji	*5:00-7:00*
げつ〜きん	getsu kara kin	*Mon-Fri*
〜をたべます	〜o tabemasu	*to eat…*
〜にいきます	〜ni ikimasu	*to go to…*

さんてんリーダー SANTEN RIIDAA **THREE-DOT LEADER** ⋯

Just as なみせん **namisen**, さんてんリーダー **santen riidaa** indicates ellipses. Additionally, it is used to indicate a special type of ellipses, suggesting unfinished thoughts or leaving readers to guess what is implied. This usage is observed with English ellipses as well. Note that **namisen** is not used for this purpose.

・・・をたべます	・・・o tabemasu	*to eat . . .*
・・・にいきます	・・・ni ikimasu	*to go to . . .*
たなかさんはいいひとで すが・・・。	Tanaka san wa ii hito desu ga…	*Mr./Ms. Tanaka is a good person but . . .*

WRITING HIRAGANA

There are slight differences in the appearance of characters between printed style and handwritten style. When practicing how to write, handwritten style must be learned. For writing practice, each character is presented within a square. The character should be always more or less centered in its square. Try following the models, and learn how to position each character in a square. Note that each large square is divided into nine smaller squares; this is to help you place your stroke accurately, just the way you learned English penmanship by using guidelines. Please note that some characters (small characters used for glides and double consonants) and some punctuation marks are centered differently depending on the direction of writing (horizontal vs. vertical). Those will be indicated accordingly. There are six blank squares provided for each character for you to practice. With enough practice, you'll be able to write without guiding squares. Don't forget: it's very important to follow the stroke order and the stroke direction of each character.

あ a

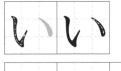

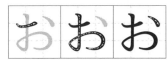

か ka

き ki

く ku

け ke

こ **ko**

さ **sa**

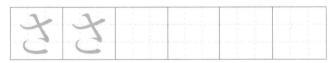

し **shi**

す **su**

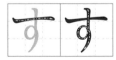

せ se

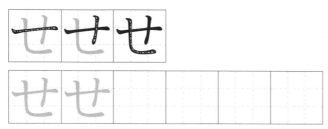

そ so

た ta

ち chi

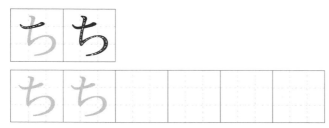

Guide to Reading and Writing Japanese

つ **tsu**

て **te**

と **to**

な **na**

に ni

ぬ nu

ね ne

の no

Guide to Reading and Writing Japanese

は ha

ひ hi

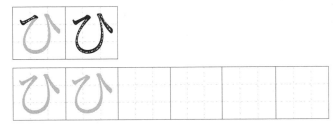

ふ fu

へ he

ほ ho

ま ma

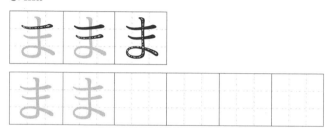

み mi

む mu

Guide to Reading and Writing Japanese

め **me**

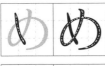

も **mo**

や **ya**

ゆ **yu**

よ **yo**

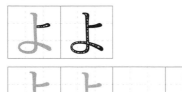

ら **ra**

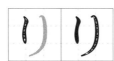

り **ri**

る **ru**

Guide to Reading and Writing Japanese

れ re

ろ ro

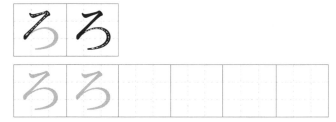

わ wa

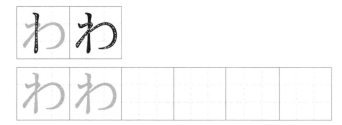

を o

ん n

が ga

ぎ gi

ぐ gu

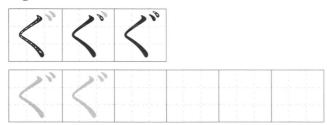

Guide to Reading and Writing Japanese

げ ge

ご go

ざ za

じ ji

ず zu

ぜ ze

ぞ zo

だ da

Guide to Reading and Writing Japanese

ぢ ji

づ zu

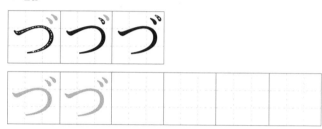

で de

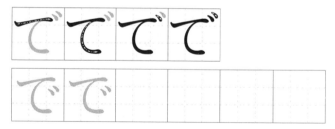

ど do

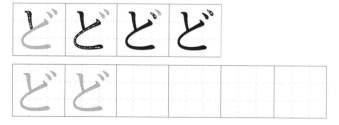

ば ba

び bi

ぶ bu

べ be

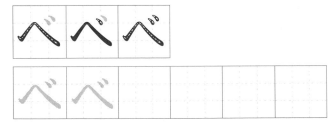

ぼ bo

ぱ pa

ぴ pi

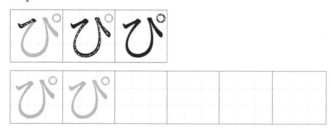

ぷ pu

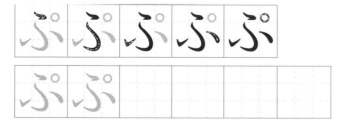

ペ pe

ぽ po

や ya (small)

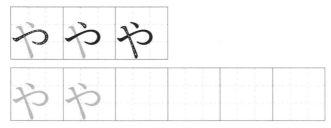

ゆ yu (small)

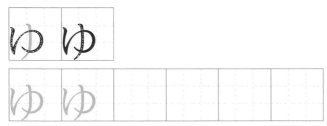

よ **yo** (small)

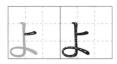

っ **tsu** (small)

や **ya** (small) (vertical)

ゆ **yu** (small) (vertical)

よ yo (small) (vertical)

っ tsu (small) (vertical)

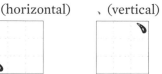

。 (horizontal)   。 (vertical)

、 (horizontal)   、 (vertical)

~ (horizontal)   ~ (vertical)

··· (horizontal)

··· (vertical)

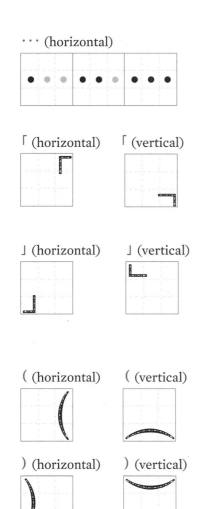

「 (horizontal)　　「 (vertical)

」 (horizontal)　　」 (vertical)

((horizontal)　　((vertical)

) (horizontal)　　) (vertical)

Part 2: Katakana

Reading Katakana

The Basic Katakana Characters
THE KATAKANA CHART

カタカナ **Katakana** characters are used mainly to write words of foreign origin, such as コンピューター **konpyuutaa** *computer* and テーブル **teeburu** *table*. Each of the 46 basic hiragana characters that you've learned has its corresponding katakana character.

カタカナのごじゅうおんひょう **Katakana no gojuuon hyoo** *The katakana chart*

	w	r	y	m	h	n	t	s	k	a	
ン n	ワ wa	ラ ra	ヤ ya	マ ma	ハ ha	ナ na	タ ta	サ sa	カ ka	ア a	**a**
		リ ri		ミ mi	ヒ hi	ニ ni	チ chi	シ shi	キ ki	イ i	**i**
		ル ru	ユ yu	ム mu	フ fu	ヌ nu	ツ tsu	ス su	ク ku	ウ u	**u**
		レ re		メ me	ヘ he	ネ ne	テ te	セ se	ケ ke	エ e	**e**
	ヲ o	ロ ro	ヨ yo	モ mo	ホ ho	ノ no	ト to	ソ so	コ ko	オ o	**o**

The use of diacritics with dakuten and handakuten, the formation of glides using small characters (ヤ, ユ, ヨ) that apply to hiragana also apply to katakana.

The use of だくてん dakuten

t	d		s	z		k	g		h	b
タ ta	ダ da		サ sa	ザ za		カ ka	ガ ga		ハ ha	バ ba
チ chi	ヂ ji		シ shi	ジ ji		キ ki	ギ gi		ヒ hi	ビ bi
ツ tsu	ヅ zu		ス su	ズ zu		ク ku	グ gu		フ fu	ブ bu
テ te	デ de		セ se	ゼ ze		ケ ke	ゲ ge		ヘ he	ベ be
ト to	ド do		ソ so	ゾ zo		コ ko	ゴ go		ホ ho	ボ bo

The use of はんだくてん handakuten

h	p
ハ ha	パ pa
ヒ hi	ピ pi
フ fu	プ pu
ヘ he	ペ pe
ホ ho	ポ po

Glides

p	b	d	z	g	r	m	h	n	t	s	k	
ピャ pya	ビャ bya	ヂャ ja	ジャ ja	ギャ gya	リャ rya	ミャ mya	ヒャ hya	ニャ nya	チャ cha	シャ sha	キャ kya	**ya**
ピュ pyu	ビュ byu	ヂュ ju	ジュ ju	ギュ gyu	リュ ryu	ミュ myu	ヒュ hyu	ニュ nyu	チュ chu	シュ shu	キュ kyu	**yu**
ピョ pyo	ビョ byo	ヂョ jo	ジョ jo	ギョ gyo	リョ ryo	ミョ myo	ヒョ hyo	ニョ nyo	チョ cho	ショ sho	キョ kyo	**yo**

Basic Katakana Characters One by One

Let's go through all the basic katakana characters one by one.

アぎょう agyoo *the A-line*	
ア a	アメリカ **amerika** *the United States*
イ i	インド **indo** *India*
ウ u	マウス **mausu** *computer mouse*
エ e	エンジン **enjin** *engine*
オ o	ラジオ **rajio** *radio*

カぎょう kagyoo *the Ka-line*	
カ ka	アメリカ **amerika** *the United States*
キ ki	キーボード **kiiboodo** *keyboard*
ク ku	クリスマス **kurisumasu** *Christmas*
ケ ke	ケーキ **keeki** *cake*
コ ko	コンピューター **konpyuutaa** *computer*

サぎょう sagyoo *the Sa-line*	
サ sa	サラダ **sarada** *salad*
シ shi	シカゴ **shikago** *Chicago*
ス su	レストラン **resutoran** *restaurant*
セ se	セーター **seetaa** *sweater*
ソ so	ソフトウエア **sofutowea** *software*

タぎょう tagyoo *the Ta-line*	
タ ta	カタカナ **katakana** *katakana*
チ chi	ブランチ **buranchi** *brunch*
ツ tsu	スポーツ **supootsu** *sports*
テ te	テニス **tenisu** *tennis*
ト to	フットボール **futtobooru** *football*

ナぎょう nagyoo *the Na-line*	
ナ na	カタカナ **katakana** *katakana*
ニ ni	モニター **monitaa** *monitor*
ヌ nu	ボジョレーヌーボー **bojoreenuuboo** *Beaujolais nouveau*
ネ ne	インターネット **intaanetto** *internet*
ノ no	ノート **nooto** *notebook*

ハぎょう hagyoo *the Ha-line*	
ハ ha	ハードウェア **haadowea** *hardware*
ヒ hi	コーヒー **koohii** *coffee*
フ fu	ナイフ **naifu** *knife*
ヘ he	ヘリコプター **herikoputaa** *helicopter*
ホ ho	ホテル **hoteru** *hotel*

Note that the katakana character ヘ **he** looks almost identical to its hiragana equivalent へ **he**.

マぎょう magyoo *the Ma-line*	
マ ma	マウス **mausu** *computer mouse*
ミ mi	ミルク **miruku** *milk*
ム mu	ゲーム **geemu** *game*
メ me	イーメール **iimeeru** *e-mail*
モ mo	モニター **monitaa** *monitor*

ヤぎょう yagyoo *the Ya-line*	
ヤ ya	タイヤ **taiya** *tire*
ユ yu	ユタ **yuta** *Utah*
ヨ yo	ヨーグルト **yooguruto** *yogurt*

ラぎょう ragyoo *the Ra-line*	
ラ ra	サラダ **sarada** *salad*
リ ri	アメリカ **amerika** *the United States*

らぎょう ragyoo *the Ra-line*	
ル ru	ホテル **hoteru** *hotel*
レ re	レストラン **resutoran** *restaurant*
ロ ro	ロンドン **rondon** *London*

Note that the katakana character リ ri looks similar to its hiragana equivalent り ri.

ワぎょう wagyoo *the Wa-line*	
ワ wa	ワイン **wain** *wine*
ヲ o	*no example*

Please note that the katakana character ヲ o is not used in everyday modern Japanese language.

And finally, just like hiragana, we have the last character ン n:

ン n	ワイン **wain** *wine*

Diacritics

Let's go through the twenty-five characters with dakuten and handakuten one by one.

ガぎょう gagyoo *the Ga-line*	
ガ ga	ガールフレンド **gaarufurendo** *girlfriend*
ギ gi	ギター **gitaa** *guitar*
グ gu	グッズ **guzzu** *goods*
ゲ ge	ゲーム **geemu** *game*
ゴ go	シカゴ **shikago** *Chicago*

ザぎょう zagyoo *the Za-line*	
ザ za	ブザー **buzaa** *buzzer*
ジ ji	ジッパー **jippaa** *zipper*
ズ zu	ポーズ **poozu** *pose*
ゼ ze	ガーゼ **gaaze** *gauze*
ゾ zo	ゾンビ **zonbi** *zombie*

ダぎょう dagyoo *the Da-line*	
ダ da	ダンス dansu *dance*
ヂ ji	ドッヂボール dojjibooru *dodgeball*
ヅ zu	*word example not available*
デ de	デリバリー deribarii *delivery*
ド do	ハードウェア haadowea *hardware*

Please note that the katakana character ヅ zu is rarely used.

バぎょう bagyoo *the Ba-line*	
バ ba	バンド bando *band*
ビ bi	ビール biiru *beer*
ブ bu	ブーツ buutsu *boots*
ベ be	ベース beesu *base*
ボ bo	ボトル botoru *bottle*

パぎょう pagyoo *the Pa-line*	
パ pa	パンダ panda *panda*
ピ pi	ピン pin *pin*
プ pu	プリント purinto *print*
ペ pe	ペン pen *pen*
ポ po	ポイント pointo *point*

Glides

Now let's go through the combination characters in katakana that create glides.

キャ kya	キャベツ kyabetsu *cabbage*
キュ kyu	キュー kyuu *cue*
キョ kyo	キョンジュ kyonju *Gyeongju (a city in South Korea)*
シャ sha	シャツ shatsu *shirt*
シュ shu	シュート shuuto *shoot*
ショ sho	ショー shoo *show*

チャ cha	チャンス chansu *chance*
チュ chu	チューリップ chuurippu *tulip*
チョ cho	チョコレート chokoreeto *chocolate*
ニャ nya	ボローニャ boroonya *Bologna (a city in Italy)*
ニュ nyu	ニュース nyuusu *news*
ニョ nyo	ニョッキ nyokki *gnocchi*
ヒャ hya	ミヒャエル mihyaeru *Michael (German pronunciation)*
ヒュ hyu	ヒューマニズム hyuumanizumu *humanism*
ヒョ hyo	*word example not available*
ミャ mya	ミャンマー myanmaa *Myanmar*
ミュ myu	ミュージカル myuujikaru *musical*
ミョ myo	*word example not available*
リャ rya	リャマ ryama *llama*
リュ ryu	リュージュ ryuuju *luge*
リョ ryo	マトリョーシカ matoryooshika *Matryoshka (Russian nesting doll)*
ギャ gya	ギャンブル gyanburu *gamble*
ギュ gyu	モンタギュー mongagyuu *Montague*
ギョ gyo	ギョウザ gyooza *gyooza dumpling*
ジャ ja	ジャズ jazu *jazz*
ジュ ju	ジュース juusu *juice*
ジョ jo	ジョギング jogingu *jogging*
ヂャ ja	*word example not available*
ヂュ ju	*word example not available*
ヂョ jo	*word example not available*
ビャ bya	*word example not available*
ビュ byu	ビューワー byuuwaa *viewer*
ビョ byo	ビョーク byooku *Björk (Icelandic name)*

ピャ pya	*word example not available*
ピュ pyu	コンピューター **konpyuutaa** *computer*
ピョ pyo	ピョンヤン **pyon-yan** *Pyongyang (a city in North Korea)*

Please note that some of these combination characters in katakana are rarely used, especially those without examples above.

Double Consonants

The rule of double consonants for katakana is the same as hiragana. Double consonants are written with a small ツ **tsu** placed immediately before the consonant to be doubled. The consonants that can be doubled are **k, s, t, c, g, z, j, d, b,** and **p** as shown in the examples below:

k	ロック **rokku** *rock or lock*
s	メッセージ **messeeji** *message*
t	マット **matto** *mat*
c	パッチ **pacchi** *patch*
g	バッグ **baggu** *bag*
z	メッゾ **mezzo** *mezzo*
f	シャッフル **shaffuru** *shuffle*
d	ベッド **beddo** *bed*
b	スノッブ **sunobbu** *snob*
p	カップ **kappu** *cup*

As noted for hiragana, keep in mind that double **n** are not considered a double consonant. This is because the first **n** is represented by the character ン **n**, as illustrated in the following examples:

| カンヌ | **kannu** | *Cannes (a city in France)* |
| トンネル | **tonneru** | *tunnel* |

Long Vowels

One major difference between hiragana and katakana usage is in the representation of long vowels. Any vowel may be elongated by writing a dash (ー) after it. Below are some examples showing the contrast between long vowels in hiragana and katakana:

hiragana word containing a long vowel			katakana word containing a long vowel		
おかあさん	okaasan	*mother (someone else's)*	スカート	**sukaato**	*skirt*
いいえ	**iie**	*no*	イーメール	**iimeeru**	*e-mail*
じゅう	**juu**	*ten*	ジュース	**juusu**	*juice*
れい	**ree**	*zero*	チョコレート	**chokoreeto**	*chocolate*
お<u>とう</u>さん	**otoosan**	*father (someone else's)*	トークシ ョー	**tookushoo**	*talk show*

Katakana-specific Combination Characters

In order to approximate the pronunciation of foreign words, the following combinations are commonly used. Note that these sound combinations are not used in hiragana.

ウィ wi	ウィンドーショッピ ング	**windooshoppingu**	*window shopping*
ウエ we	ウェイトレス	**weitoresu**	*waitress*
ウオ wo	ウォール	**wooru**	*wall*
シエ she	シェパード	**shepaado**	*shepherd*
チエ che	チェーン	**cheen**	*chain*
ティ ti	パーティー	**paatii**	*party*

ファ fa	ファックス	fakkusu	*fax*
フィ fi	フィンランド	finrando	*Finland*
フェ fe	フェンス	fensu	*fence*
フォ fo	フォーク	fooku	*fork*
ジェ je	ジェーン	jeen	*Jane*
ディ di	ディスプレイ	disupurei	*display*
デュ du	デューク	duuku	*Duke*

Remember that the second character of each of the above combinations must be written small.

おめでとうございます! **Omedetoogozaimasu!** *Congratulations!* You've learned all the basic katakana characters, diacritics, and special character combinations! In the next section, you'll learn just a couple of things to keep in mind when you read katakana; and then you'll be ready to work on some reading exercises.

READING AND PUNCTUATION RULES

Particles

Katakana is almost always used to write particular words (mainly of foreign origin) in a sentence. Therefore, you will not see the particles (such as **wa, ga, o, ni,** and **e**) written in katakana. However, if somebody chose to write those particles in katakana for a particular reason, he/she would follow the same rules that apply to hiragana. That is to use the character ハ **ha** for the particle **wa,** the character ヘ **he** for the particle **e,** and the character ヲ **o** for the particle **o.**

Punctuation

A centered dot (·) is often used between the first and the last names of foreign origin.

ジョン・スミス	jon·sumisu	John Smith

WRITING KATAKANA

As noted for hiragana, there are slight differences in the appearance of characters between typed style and handwritten style. Again, it is very important to follow the stroke order and the stroke direction of each character. There are six blank squares provided for each character for you to practice.

ア a

イ i

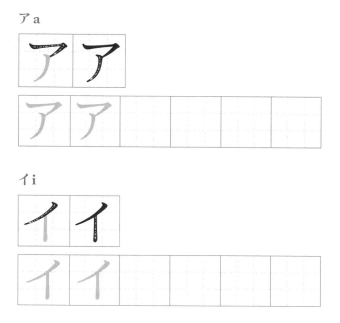

ウ u

エ e

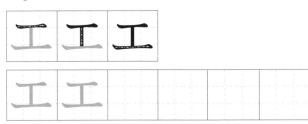

オ o

カ ka

キ ki

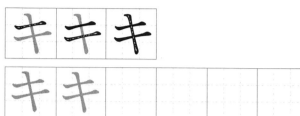

ク ku

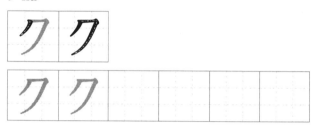

ケ ke

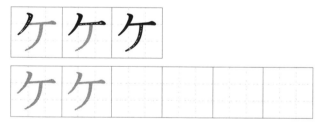

コ ko

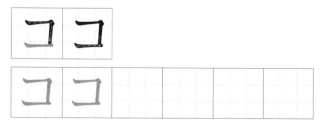

サ sa

シ shi

ス su

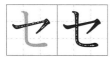

セ se

ソ so

タ ta

チ chi

ツ tsu

テ **te**

ト **to**

ナ **na**

ニ **ni**

ヌ nu

ネ ne

ノ no

ハ ha

Guide to Reading and Writing Japanese

ヒ hi

フ fu

ヘ he

ホ ho

マ **ma**

ミ **mi**

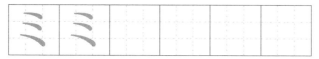

ム **mu**

メ **me**

モ mo

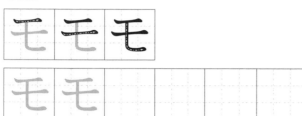

ヤ ya

ユ yu

ヨ yo

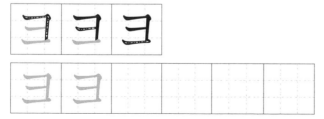

ル **ru**

ロ ro

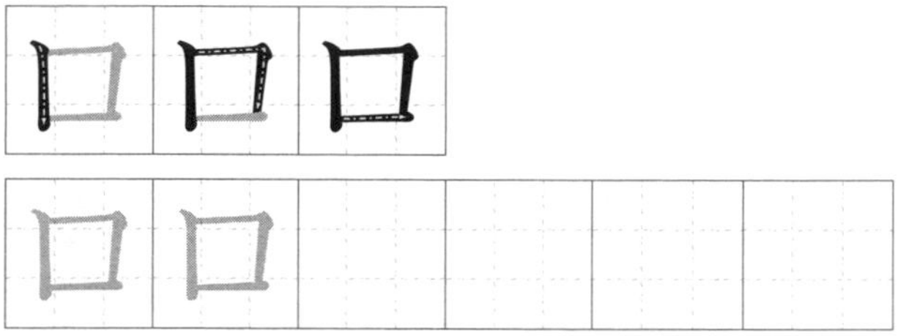

ロ ロ ロ

ロ ロ

ワ wa

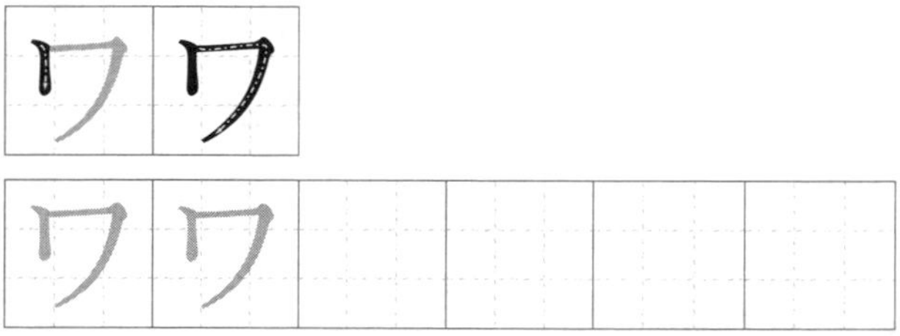

ワ ワ

ワ ワ

ヲ o

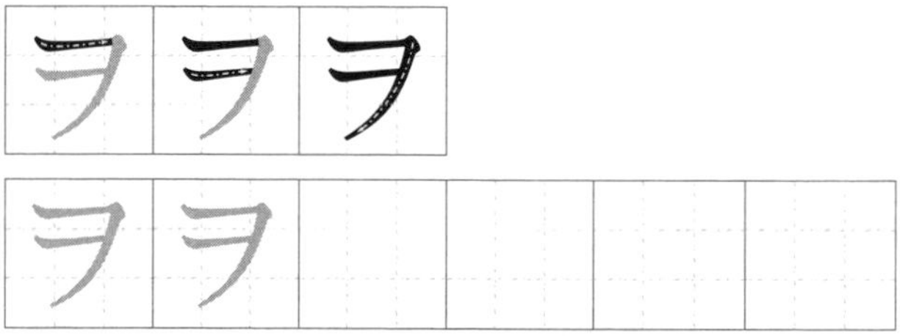

ヲ ヲ ヲ

ヲ ヲ

ン n

ン ン

ン ン

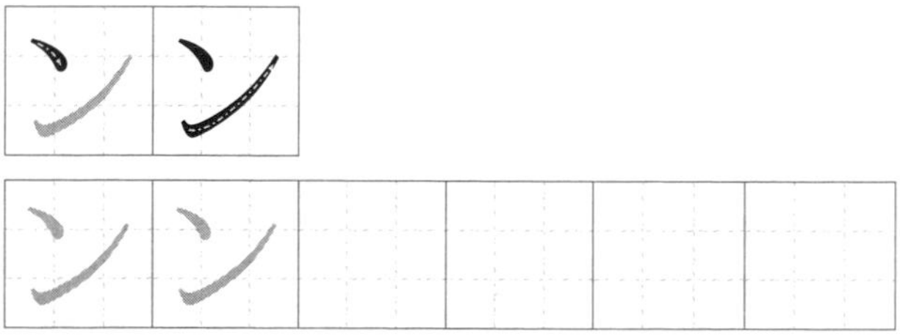

ガ ga

ギ gi

グ gu

ゲ ge

ゴ **go**

ザ **za**

ジ **ji**

ズ **zu**

ゼ **ze**

ゾ **zo**

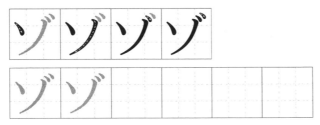

ダ **da**

チ **ji**

Guide to Reading and Writing Japanese

ヅ zu

デ de

ド do

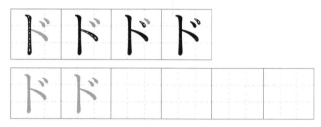

バ ba

ビ bi

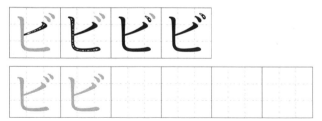

ブ bu

ベ be

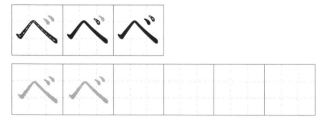

ボ bo

Guide to Reading and Writing Japanese

パ **pa**

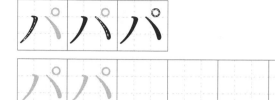

ピ **pi**

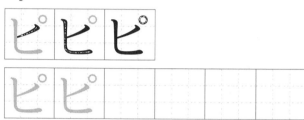

プ **pu**

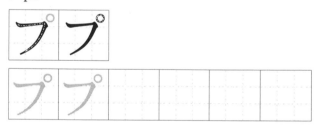

ペ **pe**

ポ po

ャ ya (small) (horizontal writing)

ャ ya (small) (vertical writing)

ユ yu (small) (horizontal writing)

ユ **yu** (small) (vertical writing)

ヨ **yo** (small) (horizontal writing)

ヨ **yo** (small) (vertical writing)

ツ **tsu** (small) (horizontal writing)

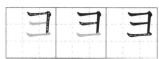

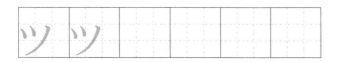

ツ tsu (small) (vertical writing)

— (dash used for a long vowel) (horizontal writing)

| (dash used for a long vowel) (vertical writing)

· (dot used for foreign names)

Part 3: Kanji

In this section of the *Guide to Reading and Writing Japanese*, we'll look at the basics of 漢字 **kanji**: some reading rules and conventions, concepts and components of kanji, and finally you'll learn how to read and write twenty very basic characters.

In *Intermediate Japanese* and *Advanced Japanese*, Japanese words and sentences are written with as many kanji characters as an average Japanese adult would use, and every kanji has 振り仮名 **furigana** over it for your reading guidance. Don't be overwhelmed by the number of characters. You are not asked to learn how to write or read all the kanji characters used in *Intermediate Japanese* and *Advanced Japanese*. They are there for you to familiarize yourself with kanji characters in action. In *Essential Japanese*, you will not see any kanji, but feel free to start studying the basic kanji in this guide once you have mastered hiragana and katakana.

READING KANJI

音読み ON YOMI (ON READING) AND 訓読み KUN YOMI (KUN READING)

There are two different types of kanji reading. One is called 音読み **on yomi** (**on** *reading*), which derived from the Chinese pronunciation. The other is called

訓読み **kun yomi** (**kun** *reading*), which is the pronunciation of the Japanese word corresponding to the meaning of the kanji character. For example, the character 水, which means *water* has the readings すい **sui** and みず **mizu**; すい **sui** is **on yomi** and みず **mizu** is **kun yomi**.

Many characters have more than one **on yomi** or **kun yomi**. For example, the character 木 which means *tree* has four readings: もく **moku**, ぼく **boku**, き **ki**, and こ **ko**. The first two are **on yomi**, and the last two are **kun yomi**.

Some characters do not have a **kun yomi**. For example, the character 茶 which means *tea* has the readings ちゃ **cha** and さ **sa**, both of which are **on yomi**, but the character does not have **kun yomi**.

Reading Rules

As a general rule, **kun yomi** is assigned when a kanji appears by itself. In contrast, when two or more kanji characters are combined to make a word, **on yomi** is assigned. Take a look at the characters 兄 and 弟 below for example.

兄		
kun yomi	あに ani	兄 ani *one's own older brother*
	にい nii	お兄さん oniisan *someone else's older brother*
on yomi	きょう kyoo	兄弟 kyoodai *siblings*
	けい kee	父兄 fukee *fathers and eldest sons*

弟		
kun yomi	おとうと otooto	弟 otooto *one's own younger brother* 弟さん otootosan *someone else's younger brother*
on yomi	だい dai	兄弟 kyoodai *siblings*
	てい tee	師弟 shitee *teacher and student* 子弟 shitee *children*
	で de	弟子 deshi *disciple*

Often a single Japanese word is written using both kanji and hiragana; for example, 行く **iku** (*to go*), 大きい **ookii** (*big*), 静か **shizuka** (*quiet*), お兄さん **oniisan** (*someone else's older brother*). The hiragana that follows kanji in a single word is called 送り仮名 **okurigana**. For example, く **ku** in 行く **iku**, きい **kii** in 大きい **ookii**, か **ka** in 静か **shizuka**, and さん **san** in お兄さん **oniisan** are okurigana. Usually, when a word has to be written with kanji and okurigana, the reading of that kanji is **kun yomi**. One major exception is the verb type 〜する … **suru** (*do …*); for example, 勉強する **benkyoosuru** (*to study*), 卒業する **sotsugyoosuru** (*to graduate*), 予約する **yoyakusuru** (*to make an appointment/reservation*). These verbs have the structure "the verb *do* + noun of Chinese origin." Since the nouns 勉強 **benkyoo** (*study*), 卒業 **sotsugyoo** (*graduation*), and 予約 **yoyaku** (*appointment/reservation*) are nouns originated in the Chinese language, **on yomi** is applied to each of the kanji characters.

ANATOMY OF KANJI

Kanji Formation

Kanji characters can be classified into four categories in terms of how they have been formed. The four categories are 象形文字 shookee moji (*pictorial characters*), 指示文字 shiji moji (*indicative characters*), 会意文字 kaii moji (*compound ideographic characters*), 形声文字 keesee moji (*phonetic-ideographic characters*). Among them, **shookee moji** and **shiji moji** are most basic, while **kaii moji** and **keesee moji** are formed by combining the basic characters.

象形文字 SHOOKEE MOJI (PICTORIAL CHARACTERS)

Shookee moji (*pictorial characters*) are originated from pictures of objects. Examples of this type of characters are shown below.

山 (*mountain*)   川 (*river*)   火 (*fire*)

指示文字 SHIJI MOJI (INDICATIVE CHARACTERS)

Shiji moji (*indicative characters*) are points and lines to express abstract concepts. Examples of this type of characters are shown below.

一 (*one*)   二 (*two*)   上 (*above, on, top*)   下 (*under, below*)

会意文字 KAII MOJI (COMPOUND IDEOGRAPHIC CHARACTERS)

Kaii moji (*compound ideographic characters*) are formed by combining **shookee moji** (*pictorial characters*) or **shiji moji** (*indicative characters*). The meaning of **kaii moji** is a result of its component characters. For example, by putting the two characters 日 (*sun*), and 月 (*moon*), we get a character 明 which means *bright*. By putting two of the character 木 (*tree*) together, we get 林 (*woods*); with three of them, we have 森 (*forest*).

形声文字 KEESEE MOJI (PHONETIC-IDEOGRAPHIC CHARACTERS)

Keesee moji (*phonetic-ideographic characters*) are also combinations of two or more simple characters. What makes **keesee moji** different from **kaii moji** is that one component represents the meaning, while the other component represents the pronunciation. It's the most complex kind of kanji but most existing kanji characters are **keesee moji**.

Now let's look at some examples. The three characters below share the same left-side component.

海 (*sea, ocean*), 湖 (*lake*), 泳 (*swim*)

The left-side component is a radical called さんずい **sanzui**. The さんずい **sanzui** radical has the meaning *water,* and thus all three characters have meanings related to water. The rest of the components in each of the characters represent various pronunciations.

Let's take a look at another set of examples. The three characters below share the same right-side component. This radical designates the **on yomi koo**. However, since the three characters have different left-side components, the meanings are unrelated.

溝 **koo** (*groove*), 講 **koo** (*lecture*), 構 **koo** (*structure*)

Radicals and Components

Let's talk more about the components of complex kanji. *Radicals* (部首 **bushu**) are the most basic components of kanji. A good knowledge of radicals is useful in understanding the composition of complex characters. Knowing radicals is sort of similar to knowing Latin and Greek roots. Just as knowing Latin and Greek roots helps to analyze and deduce the meaning of many English words, knowing radicals helps you understand many kanji characters. The number of radicals is said to be about 150 to 250.

Many radicals can traditionally be classified into seven categories, depending on their position within the character. The seven categories are presented with examples below. The radicals presented as examples here all indicate meaning rather than sound. You can see how the meaning of words is related to the meaning of the radicals.

1. 偏 **hen**: left-part radical

人偏 **ninben** (*person*)

Word that contains 人偏 **ninben**: 体 **karada** (*body*)

2. 旁 ^{つくり} tsukuri: right-part radical

力 ^{ちから} chikara (*power*)

Word that contains 力 ^{ちから} chikara: 効果 ^{こうか} kooka (*effect*)

3. 冠 ^{かんむり} kanmuri: upper-part radical

草冠 ^{くさかんむり} kusa kanmuri (*grass*)

Word that contains 草冠 ^{くさかんむり} kusa kanmuri: お茶 ^{ちゃ} ocha (*tea*)

4. 脚 ^{あし} ashi: lower-part radical

心 ^{こころ} kokoro (*heart*)

Word that contains 心 ^{こころ} kokoro (*heart*): 思う ^{おも} omou (*to think*)

5. 垂 tare: upper-and-left-part radical

病垂 yamaidare (*illness*)

Word that contains 病垂 yamaidare: 病気 byooki (*illness*)

6. 繞 nyoo: left-and-lower-part radical

しんにょう/しんにゅう shinnyoo/shinnyuu (*proceed*)

Word that contains しんにょう/しんにゅう shinnyoo/shinnyuu: 近い chikai (*near*)

7. 構 kamae: outer-portion radical

国構 **kunigamae** (*country*)

Word that contains 国構 **kunigamae**: 国 **kuni** (*country*)

WRITING KANJI

In this section, you will learn how to write twenty very basic kanji characters. Each of these characters cannot be broken down into simpler kanji.

By now, you should be familiar with 仮名 **kana** stroke order. When you learn kanji, you need to learn how many strokes each character takes to write, and also the order of strokes. It sounds like arduous work, but it is certainly rewarding in the end because it will in fact make learning and writing characters easier, especially the more complex ones. Knowing exactly how many strokes it takes to write a kanji character is particularly important because you need to know this in order to look up words in a kanji dictionary. There are some general principles in stroke order, which can come in handy; although there are some exceptions, generally each character is written from left to right, top to bottom, and horizontal lines before vertical lines. It's useful to remember the following Japanese expressions: 画 **kaku** (*stroke*), 画数 **kakusuu** (*number of strokes*), 書き順 **kakijun** (*stroke order*).

Just as with kana, you should follow the handwritten style when you practice writing kanji because there are subtle differences between the handwritten style and the typed style.

一 *One*		
kun yomi	ひと hito	一つ hitotsu *one*
on yomi	いち ichi	一月 ichigatsu *January*
	いつ itsu	同一 dooitsu *identical*

二 *Two*		
kun yomi	ふた futa	二つ futatsu *two*
on yomi	に ni	二月 nigatsu *February*

三 *Three*		
kun yomi	み(つ) mi	三つ mittsu *three*
on yomi	さん san	三月 sangatsu *March*

四 *Four*		
kun yomi	よ(つ) yo	四つ yottsu *four*
	よん yon	四分 yonpun *four minutes*
on yomi	し shi	四月 shigatsu *April*

四 四 四 四 四

四 四

五 *Five*		
kun yomi	いつ itsu	五つ itsutsu *five*
on yomi	ご go	五月 gogatsu *May*

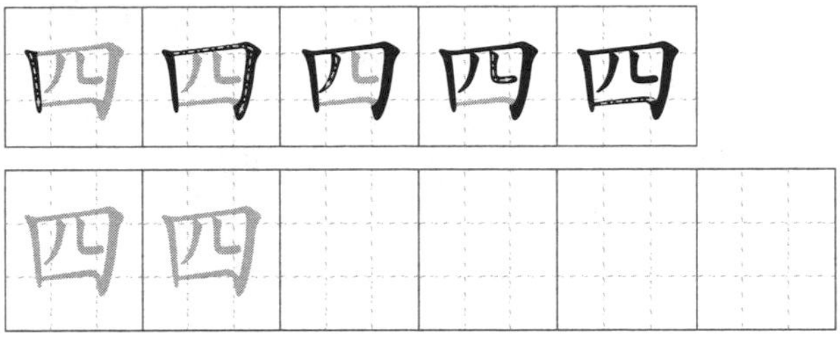

五 五 五 五

五 五

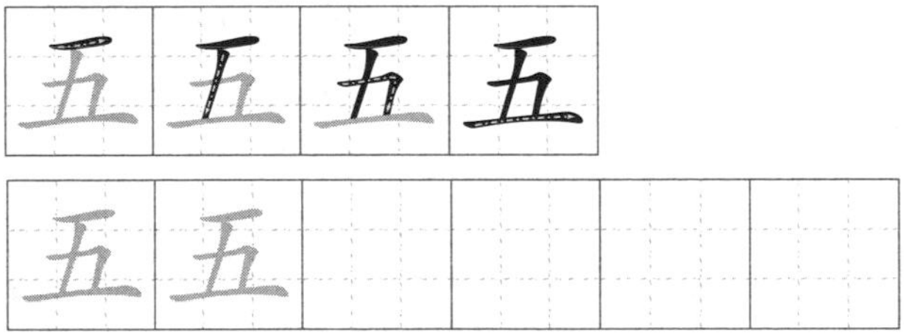

六 *Six*		
kun yomi	む(つ) mu	六つ muttsu *six*
on yomi	ろく roku	六月 rokugatsu *June*

七 *Seven*		
kun yomi	なな nana	七つ nanatsu *seven*
on yomi	しち shichi	七月 shichigatsu *July*

八 *Eight*		
kun yomi	や(つ) ya	八つ yattsu *eight*
on yomi	はち hachi	八月 hachigatsu *August*

九 *Nine*		
kun yomi	ここの kokono	<ruby>九<rt>ここの</rt></ruby>つ kokonotsu *nine*
on yomi	きゅう kyuu	<ruby>九人<rt>きゅうにん</rt></ruby> kyuunin *nine people*
	く ku	<ruby>九月<rt>く がつ</rt></ruby> kugatsu *September*

十 *Ten*		
kun yomi	とお too	<ruby>十<rt>とお</rt></ruby> too *ten*
on yomi	じゅう juu	<ruby>十月<rt>じゅうがつ</rt></ruby> juugatsu *October*

大 *Big*		
kun yomi	おお oo	<ruby>大<rt>おお</rt></ruby>きい **ookii** *big*
on yomi	だい dai	<ruby>大学<rt>だいがく</rt></ruby> **daigaku** *college, university*
	たい tai	<ruby>大切<rt>たいせつ</rt></ruby> **taisetsu** *important*

小 *Small*		
kun yomi	ちい chii	<ruby>小<rt>ちい</rt></ruby>さい **chiisai** *small*
	こ ko	<ruby>小麦<rt>こむぎ</rt></ruby> **komugi** *wheat*
	お o	<ruby>小川<rt>おがわ</rt></ruby> **ogawa** *stream*
on yomi	しょう shoo	<ruby>小学校<rt>しょうがっこう</rt></ruby> **shoogakkoo** *elementary school*

小 小 小

小 小

人 Person		
kun yomi	ひと hito	おんな ひと 女の人 onna no hito *female*
on yomi	じん jin	に ほんじん 日本人 nihonjin *Japanese (person)*
	にん nin	さんにん 三人 sannin *three people*

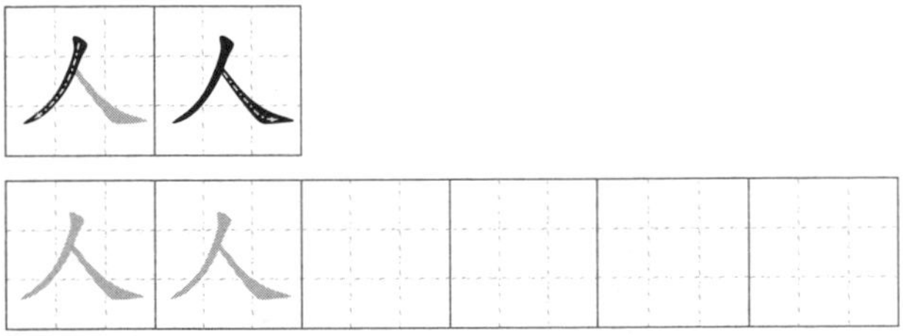

人 人

人 人

月 Moon		
kun yomi	つき tsuki	つき 月 tsuki *moon*
on yomi	げつ getsu	げつよう び 月曜日 getsuyoobi *Monday*
	がつ gatsu	いちがつ 一月 ichigatsu *January*

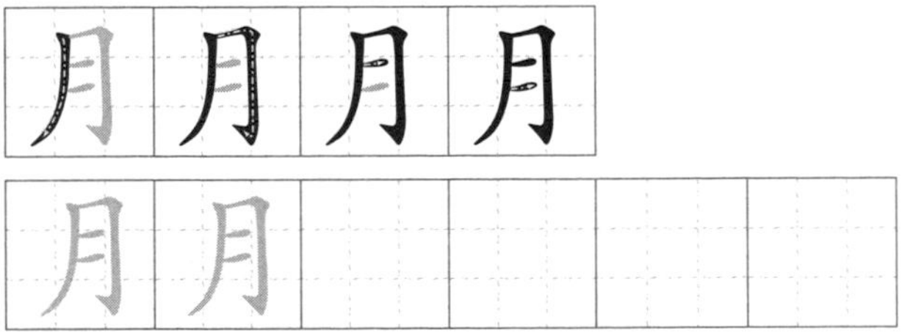

月 月 月 月

月 月

火 Fire		
kun yomi	ひ hi	火 hi *fire*
on yomi	か ka	火曜日 kayoobi *Tuesday*

火 火 火 火

火 火

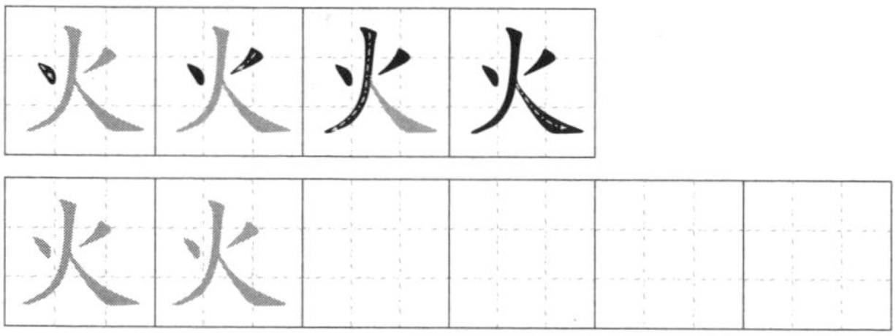

水 Water		
kun yomi	みず mizu	水 mizu *water*
on yomi	すい sui	水曜日 suiyoobi *Wednesday*

水 水 水 水

水 水

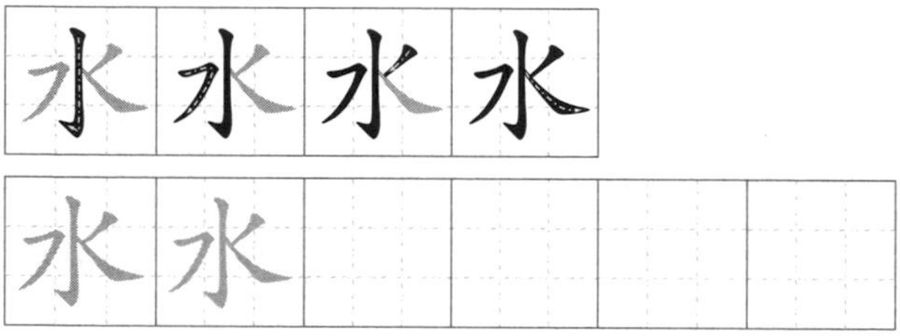

木 *Tree*		
kun yomi	き ki	木 ki *tree*
	こ ko	木かげ kokage *tree shadow*
on yomi	もく moku	木曜日 mokuyoobi *Thursday*
	ぼく boku	大木 taiboku *big tree*

金 *Gold*		
kun yomi	かね kane	お金 okane *money*
on yomi	きん kin	金曜日 kinyoobi *Friday*
	こん kon	金色 konjiki *golden color*

土 Soil, earth

kun yomi	つち tsuchi	^{つち}土 tsuchi *soil*
on yomi	ど do	^{どようび}土曜日 doyoobi *Saturday*
	と to	^{とち}土地 tochi *land*

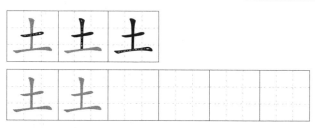

日 Day, sun

kun yomi	ひ hi	^{ちち ひ}父の日 chichi no hi *father's day*
	び bi	^{げつようび}月曜日 getsuyoobi *Monday*
	か ka	^{みっか}三日 mikka *third day, three days*
on yomi	にち nichi	^{まいにち}毎日 mainichi *every day*
	に ni	^{にほん}日本 nihon *Japan*
	じつ jitsu	^{せんじつ}先日 senjitsu *the other day*

日曜日 NICHIYOBI SUNDAY